PICASSO
and his art

'More than all poets, sculptors
and other artists, this Spaniard
leaves us breathless . . . His obstinate
pursuit of beauty has guided his
steps, making him in morality a
Latin but in rhythm an Arab.'

Guillaume Apollinaire, 1905

PICASSO
and his art

Denis Thomas

Galahad Books New York

Frontispiece
The Three Musicians
1921
oil on canvas
80 × 74 in (203 × 188 cm)
Philadelphia Museum of Art, Pennsylvania
(A. E. Gallatin Collection)

Published by Galahad Books
a division of A & W Promotional Books Corporation
95 Madison Avenue, New York, NY 10016

Library of Congress Catalog Card No. 74–78014
ISBN 0–88365–175–7

© Copyright The Hamlyn Publishing Group 1975

Phototypeset in England by
Filmtype Services Limited, Scarborough
Printed in Spain by
Mateu Cromo Artes Gráficas S.A., Madrid

Contents

than the *dramatis personae* of the Blue Period, partly because of this subtle realism and partly because they still leave the everyday issues of human relations unresolved; the underlying tensions and anxieties remain, with Harlequin himself incapable of helping outside his theatrical *persona*. Picasso often shows him as a neutered figure, neither male nor female. His potency is not physical: perhaps, like his act, it is just a trick. In the curiously beautiful *Family of Acrobats with an Ape* (plate 17) he has even lost the gay, protective diamonds of his costume, so that he recedes from the family group in pale tones. The focal point is the twisting child, sitting on the lap made by the young mother lifting her right heel – a movement echoed by that of Harlequin, whose tender gaze is

Plate 16
The Family of Saltimbanques
1905
oil on canvas
84 × 90¼ in (213 × 231 cm)
National Gallery of Art, Washington, D.C.
(Chester Dale Collection)

Plate 17
Family of Acrobats with an Ape
1905
gouache on cardboard
40 × 28¾ in (104 × 75 cm)
Konstmuseum, Göteborg

26

matched, incongruously but very movingly, by that of the ape.

As so often with Picasso, precedents abound in earlier works of art: the ape has been depicted as a companion of clowns and jesters since medieval times, and there exists an engraving by Dürer showing a Madonna with a monkey which Picasso might have known through copies. Again, he liked to keep a monkey in his studio, and was to introduce one in his late drawings and etchings as an ironic *alter ego*. That he saw himself as Harlequin, and shared his role in the human comedy, is also obvious from the element of self-portraiture, culminating in *At the Lapin Agile*, painted in 1905. Picasso shows himself as a disconsolate Harlequin at a bar, in the same relationship to a nearby woman as Harlequin often appears with his wife, aware but separate. This painting hung in the Lapin Agile, Montmartre, and was well known to denizens of the quarter. Eugène Marsan made mention of it in a novel, *Sandricourt*, published a year later: 'They aren't even looking at one another, yet we know they are lovers. The man who splashed them on to canvas in a couple of hours will become a genius—if Paris doesn't murder him first . . . You had better learn his name. It is Picasso.'

When Picasso laid Harlequin to rest he did so in gouache

Plate 18
The Death of Harlequin
1905
gouache on board
26 × 36½ in (66 × 93 cm)
Collection of Mr and Mrs Paul Mellon

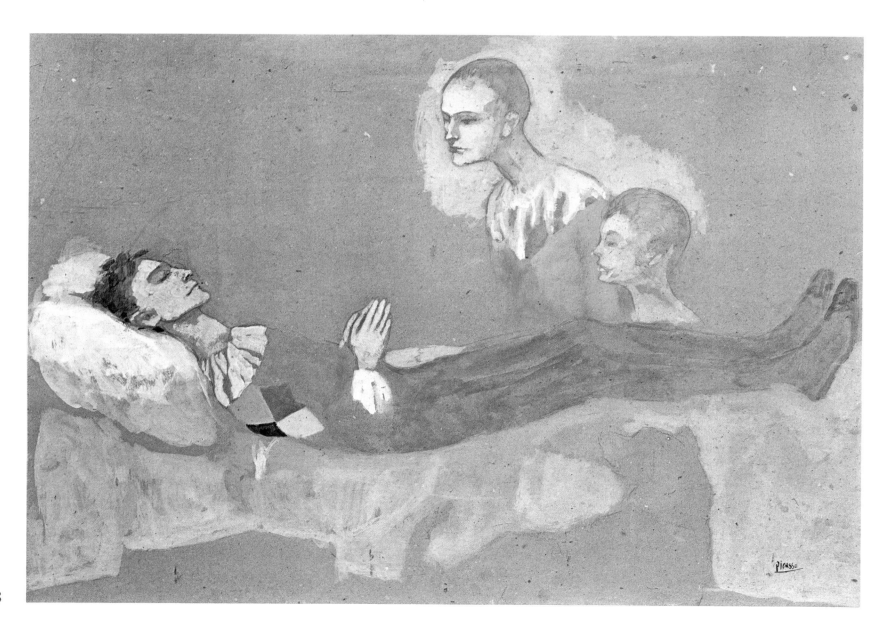

28

43

like and sinister, raising unanswerable questions about the nature of the music which the three strange companions have sat down to play.

The disaster which his friends had foreseen when Picasso confronted them with *Les Demoiselles d'Avignon* had not come to pass. Instead Cubism had given rise to a virtual school of painting, with Picasso and Braque at its head and with painters of the calibre of Gris, Léger, Picabia, Delaunay, Derain and Duchamp among its most passionate adherents. Two other painters, who had exhibited with this group at the Salon des Indépendants in 1911, published a book on Cubism as early as 1912. They were followed by Apollinaire's *Les Peintres Cubistes* a year later, in which he wrote of Cubism as the most audacious school of painting which had ever appeared, 'raising anew the

Plate 32
Still-Life with Fruit
1917
oil on canvas
15¾ × 11 in (40 × 28 cm)
Museo Picasso, Barcelona

44

whole question of what is beautiful'. Picasso, he noted, 'studies an object as a surgeon dissects a corpse'—a remark which, though often quoted, discounts the essential life-force which made Picasso declare that 'there is no such thing as *nature morte*.' It was Apollinaire, too, who as editor of the review *Les Soirées de Paris*, first reproduced Picasso's constructions (which have long since been dismantled or fallen apart) made from the 'mean, soiled, despised' materials described by Aragon. So many subscribers indignantly cancelled their subscriptions that Apollinaire lost his job.

Though Picasso's life continued for a while in the cheerfully bohemian manner of his early years in Paris, his emergence as the leading young painter of his time attracted the attention of a wider society than the band of poets, writers, entertainers, talkers and fellow immigrants who surrounded him. Fernande Olivier, who

Plate 33
Parade
1917
costume design for the ballet
gouache
$10\frac{3}{4} \times 7\frac{3}{8}$ in (27.3 × 18.7 cm)
Jacques Helft Collection, Paris

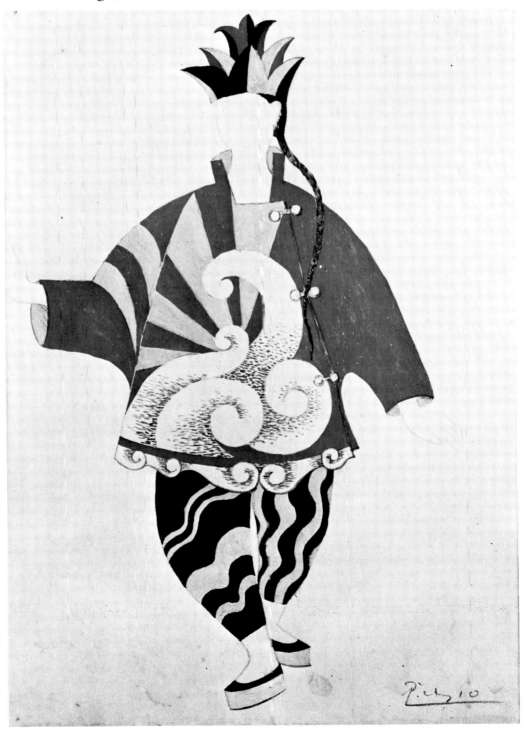

45

Plate 34
Little Girl with a Hoop
1919
oil on canvas
$12\frac{5}{8} \times 8\frac{1}{4}$ in (32.1 × 21 cm)
Musée National d'Art Moderne, Paris

Plate 35
The Three-cornered Hat
1919
pencil study for drop curtain for the ballet
Collection of the artist

Plate 36
Portrait of Igor Stravinsky
1920
pencil
$24\frac{1}{2} \times 30\frac{3}{4}$ in (62 × 48 cm)
Collection of the artist

had lived through the hard times with him, slipped from his life. Some of the early Cubist paintings of 1911–12 inscribed 'Eva' or 'Ma Jolie' (plate 30) are dedications to her successor, Marcelle Humbert. She was to play only a brief role in Picasso's life, for she died in January 1916. Picasso's friends joined him at her funeral, an event which one of them, the painter Juan Gris, described in a letter as 'a very sad affair, and Max's jokes added enormously to the horror of it'. The anti-German feeling among Parisians made itself felt in Picasso's circle. The German-born dealer Kahnweiler, exiled in Switzerland, had been the first to exhibit Cubist paintings, so that Cubism was initially regarded as a kind of anti-patriotic demonstration masquerading as art. (Kahnweiler's entire collection, and that of the critic and collector Wilhelm Uhde, another of Picasso's patrons, was subsequently seized by the French government and put up for auction.) The first performance of the Cubist ballet *Parade*, in May 1917, was greeted with shouts of '*Sales Boches!*' – the most bitter of insults in wartime Paris. Only the conspicuous presence of Apollinaire, in uniform, heavily bandaged around the head from a shrapnel wound and sporting his Croix de Guerre, kept the audience's feelings of patriotic outrage in check.

One consequence of Picasso's association with the Ballets Russes was his falling in love with the young dancer Olga Koklova. When Diaghilev's season in Paris ended and he took the company to Madrid and Barcelona, Picasso followed, to be warmly welcomed after his five years' absence by his family and friends. Diaghilev then took the company to South America; and Olga stayed behind with Picasso. They married in Paris in July 1918, with Apollinaire, Max Jacob and Jean Cocteau as witnesses. Picasso's new-found happiness was suddenly shattered when, on Armistice Day 1918, Guillaume Apollinaire died in hospital, a victim of his wounds and of the influenza epidemic. No friend of his youth was more dear to Picasso, or dared more in his defence. Picasso told his friend and biographer Roland Penrose how Apollinaire, dying in his hospital bed, heard the crowds outside shouting 'Hang Guillaume!' His wife (they had married only that summer) reassured him that the cries were not for him, but for the Kaiser.

Picasso's first portrait of Olga, painted in Barcelona before their marriage, shows her in a Spanish mantilla, wearing a grave and womanly expression which he has set down with obvious tenderness. Though this was to be one of his last naturalistic portraits in oils, the classic principles of form and line co-existed with whatever style preoccupied him at any particular time. His drawings reveal this mastery of traditional draughtsmanship even more vividly than his paintings. His pencil portraits of Max Jacob (1915), of Apollinaire in his conscript's uniform (1916), of Diaghilev (1917) and of Stravinsky (1920, plate 36) are all masterpieces of line drawing comparable with Ingres or any other of his French predecessors.

This genius for portraiture belonged to him from childhood; at the Museo Picasso in Barcelona, sketchbooks dating from his thirteenth year show an unerring understanding of his subjects, usually members of his family. In his early days in Barcelona and Paris he would amuse himself by drawing, upside down, the companion facing him across a café table. His astonished sitter would see his likeness appear as if by magic on the piece of paper which the artist, without bothering to turn it round, passed across to him. When the critic Félix Fénéon was brought by Apollinaire to see *Les Demoiselles d'Avignon*, all he could find to say was that Picasso ought to go in for caricature. Picasso later remarked that this was not such bad advice, since all good portraits are to some extent caricatures. He frequently introduces this element into what is, on the face of it, a perfectly serious piece of work. His

Plate 37
Three Dancers
1919–20
pencil
$10\frac{3}{8} \times 15\frac{1}{2}$ in (26.3 × 39.5 cm)
Collection of the artist

Plate 38
Pierrot and Harlequin Serenading
1918
pencil
$10\frac{1}{4} \times 7\frac{1}{2}$ in (26 × 19 cm)
Art Institute of Chicago, Illinois
(Gift of Mrs Gilbert W. Chapman)

Plate 39
Mother and Child
1921
oil on canvas
56½ × 64 in (143 × 162 cm)
Art Institute of Chicago, Illinois

strong pencil drawing, *Three Dancers* (1919–20, plate 37), though infused with the femininity of a classical *pas de trois*, shows the dancers as muscular, earth-bound young women who would shake the stage they landed on. In *Pierrot and Harlequin Serenading* (1918, plate 38) the drawing is wholly sympathetic, the stylised contortions of the clown with his fiddle being part of his traditional role.

Picasso's life with Olga was for a time rich in satisfactions. His work, always to a large extent autobiographical, took on an even deeper expressiveness as his innate love of womankind flowed out in a series of nobly massive nudes. His son Paul, born in 1921, figures in numerous paintings and drawings of the next few years,

Plate 40
Mother and Child
1922
oil on canvas
$39\frac{1}{2} \times 31\frac{1}{2}$ in (100 × 80 cm)
Baltimore Museum of Art, Maryland
(The Cone Collection)

releasing not only Picasso's delight in the experience of fatherhood but also a sense of classical continuity inspired by his contented marriage. The *Mother and Child* of 1921 (plate 39) has a rough-hewn, monumental quality which puts it among the most impressive paintings of the period. A version of the same subject (plate 40) painted a year later, now in Baltimore, achieves a classical combination of form and line extraordinary even in Picasso. In both paintings the mother, tender but impassive, seems withdrawn into a private world where no painter may intrude. In 1924, at the age of three, Paul appears as Harlequin (plate 41). A year later he is Pierrot. Neither painting can be said to owe anything to Cubism: the mood and manner are tender, catching a child's serious pleasure in dressing up. Twenty-five years later, painting another infant son, Claude, with his hobbyhorse (plate 78), Picasso enters into the heart of a little boy's world by simulating a child's painting: a marvel of imaginative identification which turns a *jeu d'esprit* into a work of art.

The sunny, languorous Mediterranean coast where Picasso and Olga spent five successive summers inspired a series of paintings looking from their balcony, and of *guéridons* (still-lifes on pedestal tables), which blaze with a southern light (plates 42, 43). It pours in from all sides, suffusing even solid forms, while the blue sea glints and beckons beyond the wide-open windows. These summers, in a landscape which Picasso immediately claimed as his own, stirred in him the Attic sensuality which dignifies his studies of bathers at this time (plate 44), and the latent folk-memory of fauns, centaurs and other creatures who inhabit the secret places of the mind.

Picasso during the early 1920s was still immersed in the world of the ballet (plate 45), which offered him the chance to use the language of both Cubism and classicism in a three-dimensional form. Diaghilev invited him to design the décor for a wholly original ballet with music by Erik Satie, called *Mercure*, in collaboration with Picasso's admired friend Leonid Massine, who was to dance–or, more strictly, mime–the principal role. Satie described the ballet as having a subject but no plot. 'It is a purely decorative spectacle, and you may imagine Picasso's marvellous contribution, which I have attempted to interpret musically.' The scenes, in the form of variations on the legend of Mercury in such roles as the lover of Venus, messenger of the gods and companion of Bacchus, included some which were thought to be provocatively shocking, such as the Three Graces being played by men in wigs with huge red painted breasts. As the ballet never found a regular place in Diaghilev's repertoire, the public at large were not given a chance to pass an opinion. It was critically received and probably misunderstood except by such spirits as the Surrealist leader André Breton and his friends, who contributed a jointly signed article to a Paris newspaper expressing their whole-hearted admiration for Picasso, who they said 'goes on creating a disturbing modernity at the highest level of expression'.

The Surrealists' high regard for Picasso arose from their recognising in his work the daring flights of intuitive fancy which André Breton called 'pure psychic automatism', the means of expressing the true process of thought free from the exercise of reason. It already had a long pedigree when Breton took over the term *surréaliste* from Apollinaire He admired Picasso's constructions and innovations in collage, and when the first issue of *La Révolution Surréaliste* appeared at the end of 1924 it included a reproduction of one of Picasso's reliefs. The fourth issue, in July 1925, contained Breton's article, *Le Surréalisme et la Peinture*, with

Plate 41
Harlequin
Paul at the Age of Three
1924
oil on canvas
51¼ × 38¼ in (130 × 97 cm)
Private collection

exhibition at the Museum of Modern Art; and there, except for being shown again in Europe in 1955, it has remained. Despite feelers from the Franco government, Picasso refused to allow *Guernica* to be taken to Spain so long as the regime remained in power. No doubt his wishes will be respected. *Guernica* lives on as a testament which somehow makes its terrible truths more bearable, sublimating the pain and embodying the pity. Attempts to find metaphors in it have foundered on the simple fact that it is a work of art. One scholar who sought Picasso's assent to his interpretation of the horse as standing for Spanish nationalism, and the bull as standing for the Spanish people, was shortly answered. 'This bull', said Picasso 'is a bull, and this horse is a horse . . . The public who look at the picture must see in the horse and the bull symbols which they interpret as they understand them. It's up to the public to see what it wants to see.'

After the concentrated agonies of *Guernica*, Picasso left Paris for the easy-going Mediterranean resort of Mougins, taking Dora Maar with him. Her intelligent good looks and vivacious conversation helped to keep her at the centre of Picasso's circle, several members of which joined the couple at their hotel for the summer. Picasso's portraits of his new mistress reflect his delight in her brilliant eyes, elegant hands and vividly bow-shaped mouth. Humorous, half-mocking portraits of his friend Eluard and others

Plate 59
Goat Skull and Bottle
1951–52
painted bronze
height 31 in (78.7 cm)
Museum of Modern Art, New York
(Mrs Simon Guggenheim Fund)

also express a lifting of Picasso's spirits in the benign warmth of sun and good fellowship. But the continuing miseries of Spain still made their demands. In a number of studies of women weeping (plate 63), Picasso reverts to images of grief, using a woman's face to express in merciless close-up the helpless disintegration which is the extremity of mental pain. The sharp, jagged lines, hysterically interlocked, the eyes cancelled out with black crosses, the tears painted as needles: these are the means by which Picasso involves the spectator, drawing short, hard lines from the centre of the subject to the springs of our own emotion.

The Minotaur makes a return appearance, though with a less bestial face than in the glowering presence of the *Minotauromachia*; and in the early months of 1938 Picasso sums up the intensity of the times in a series of still-lifes in which a simple orange turns into a glowing sun, seeming to melt the jug which stands beside it. In another strikingly vivid work of this time, *Woman with a Cockerel*, Picasso seems to identify the woman with the trussed victim on her lap; they both have the same mindless vacuity, which dehumanises the woman but gives a weird identity to the bird. A facial likeness to Picasso himself nevertheless comes through, contributing yet another element of uneasiness.

Picasso's portraits of Marie-Thérèse and of Dora Maar (plate 64) in 1937 and 1938 show them almost full face and at the same time in profile, as if the sitter had turned her head at the instant the likeness was created. The same effect is apparent in a portrait of his little daughter Maïa with a sailor doll (plate 65), in which she is given the woman's face which she will one day inherit from her mother. The contorted angles of the legs and feet describe the seemingly boneless postures of babyhood. In other paintings of

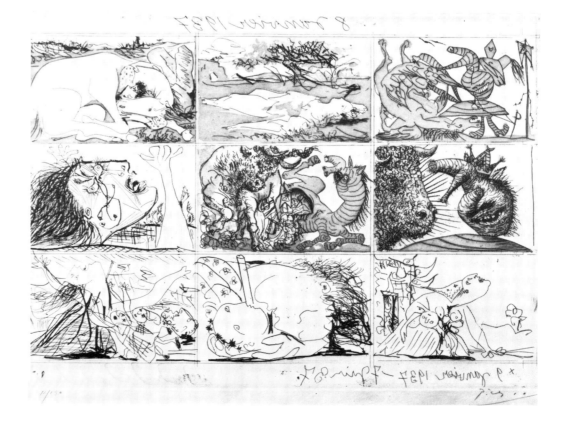

this time the cockerel reappears, stridently coloured and uttering the open-mouthed cries familiar from Picasso's earlier symbolic victim, the horse. ('There have always been cocks,' he said, 'but like everything else in life we must discover them, just as Corot discovered the morning, and Renoir discovered girls.')

Such images, evoking a kind of poetic violence, seem inseparable from Picasso's restless imagination. Poetry, indeed, is at the heart of his intelligence no less than of his painting. There are passages in his curiously disturbing play, *The Four Little Girls*, which achieve in words the sustained flights that he demonstrates in paint. Colour, as a vehicle of emotion, is used literally in passages which flash like brush-strokes: 'You mustn't believe that the cat has gone off behind the carrots to eat its eagle without fear or remorse. The blue of its cry for pity, the mauve of its leaps and the violent violets of its claws tearing Veronese-green rays from the sulphur yellow of its rage, detached from the blood spurting from the fountain full of vermilion, the ochre of the lilac wall and the sharp cobalt fringes of its cries, the poor bird crouching on the clogs of its feathers, acrobatic monkey, the flags smacking their tongues on the steel and the knife already embedded . . .'

The girls' conversations are soaked in colour; their vocabulary, even in translation, shimmers with light: 'I would like to have a gold violet silk dress embroidered with silver, sewn with pearls, jasmin and gossamer, bordered with branches of mimosa, helio-trope, narcissi, carnations, ears of corn and my head surrounded in flames seen between the brambles . . .'

Through the words, actions and imaginings of the little girls Picasso discloses the cruelty which lies just below the surface

Plate 60
The Dream and Lie of Franco
1937
etching and aquatint
$23\frac{1}{4} \times 15\frac{7}{8}$ in (59.1 × 40.3 cm)
Collection of Sir Roland Penrose

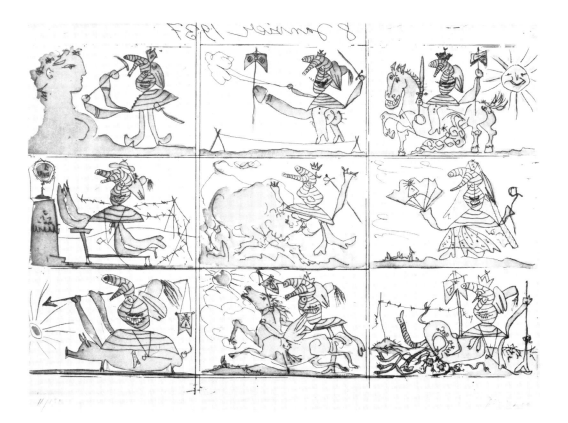

of innocence – though, as usual, with no hint of a comment or position of his own. His little girls embody the spitefulness as well as the joys of childhood: 'Let us open all the roses with our nails and make their perfumes bleed on the wrinkles of fire . . . Let's play at hurting ourselves and hug each other with fury making horrible noises,' exclaims one of them. Whereupon a second calls: 'Mummy, Mummy, come and see Yvette ransacking the garden and setting the butterflies on fire!' Roland Penrose, whose translation this is, has remarked on Picasso's lifelong humility before the wonder of children's vision. In the play, the children, like Picasso himself, are 'exploring the illusions and realities of a new world.'

News of atrocities in Spain, and the accelerating crisis in Europe, prompted Picasso to find a new metaphor for cruelty: a cat, in whose cruel jaws a ripped and bleeding bird struggles with death (plate 66). The cat's claws, spread like hooked thorns, and its baleful semi-human face turn the familiar pet into a fearsome predator. In a similar response to the onrush of war, Picasso subjected the face and body of Dora Maar to a series of derangements which have the quality of nightmares. They culminate in a portrait in which she appears to be combing her hair in a hurricane, her physical components shattered into splinters rearranged as jagged cubes. The portrait tells us nothing about Dora Maar; it speaks only of Picasso.

In the last few weeks before Hitler's invasion of Poland, Picasso painted his largest picture since *Guernica*: *Night Fishing at Antibes* (plate 67), now in the Museum of Modern Art, New York. It is an improvisation on the theme of night fishing in the harbour of

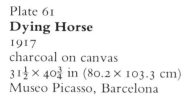

Plate 61
Dying Horse
1917
charcoal on canvas
$31\frac{1}{2} \times 40\frac{3}{4}$ in (80.2 × 103.3 cm)
Museo Picasso, Barcelona

Plate 62
Guernica
1937
oil on canvas
138 × 308 in (289 × 782 cm)
Museum of Modern Art, New York
(on extended loan from the artist's
collection)

Antibes, the men leaning over the sides of their boat to spear fish
attracted by the glow of the kerosene lamp in the prow, watched
by two girls on the harbour wall. The whole is suffused with a
luminous submarine light which gives it a dreamlike intensity.
The towers of the Grimaldi Palace gleam in the night sky, and the
light of stars explodes in the soft air. When Hitler invaded Poland
a few weeks later, Picasso took the painting with him to Paris,
rolled up on the back seat of his Hispano motor car. It would be
six years before he set eyes on the Mediterranean again.

France was yet to fall. When it did, and as German troops
marched into Royan, the small resort south of Bordeaux where
Picasso and his ménage had by now taken refuge, he painted his
Nude Dressing Her Hair (plate 68). It is an almost unbearably painful
picture, more so even than the *Portrait of Dora Maar* (plate 64),
since it contains a sensuality which stirs feelings of repugnance
rather than of pity. The parts are related to one another only by
memory; the zones of erotic pleasure are chopped up as if on a
butcher's slab. Sabartés, who had rejoined Picasso, has told how
they watched as the troops filed past. Picasso said: 'Basically, if
you look carefully, they are very stupid. So many troops, so many
machines, so much power, so much turmoil, just to get here.
We arrived with much less fuss. Such stupidity! Why can't they
behave like us?'

As a public enemy of Fascism, Picasso had nothing to look
forward to under the Nazis. As an artist, he represented all that
the Aryan cult most feared and detested, *Kunstbolschewismus*, the

acme of non-Aryan degeneration. His closest friends included Jewish and Communist artists, writers and intellectuals. In New York, his great anti-Fascist testament was drawing the crowds to an important retrospective exhibition at the Museum of Modern Art. He had every reason, and every opportunity, to flee the country. But Picasso was in no doubt where he should be: in Paris, at the centre of whatever was to come. The Nazis left him alone, except to offer extra rations of food and coal in exchange for public displays of goodwill. Picasso refused. Sadly for France, and for the civilised world, there were not lacking prominent French intellectuals ready to join the invaders in deriding those with the

courage to stand firm. Picasso, though not prevented from working was forbidden to exhibit. Instead, his friends called on him to view and discuss his pictures. His visitors sometimes included the Gestapo. On one such visit a Nazi officer noticed a reproduction of *Guernica* lying on a table. 'Did you do this?' he asked. 'No,' replied Picasso. 'You did.'

Throughout the Occupation, the studio in the Rue des Grands Augustins, where Picasso had settled in preference to the Rue la Boëtie, represented for his friends and supporters the private resistance of the mind. Picasso, driven in on himself, turned again to writing. In the space of four days early in 1941, he finished a play which he called *Le Désir Attrapé par la Queue* ('Desire Caught by the Tail'), written in a style of sardonic fantasy and full of references to the privations of the times. It tells of a poet, Big Foot, who lives with his artist friend Onion, who is also his rival for the favours of The Tart. With other weirdly named members of their circle they take part in surrealistic conversations and events in which the dominant themes are bodily comforts, notably food,

Plate 65
Portrait of Maïa with a Doll
1938
oil on canvas
$28\frac{3}{4} \times 23\frac{1}{2}$ in (73 × 60 cm)
Private collection

(plate 90) with Jacqueline again in the leading role as the odalisque figure. The dominant male, adapted from the man lounging on the right of Manet's group with a cane in his hand, becomes in Picasso's version a narrator, holding his companions' attention with talk and gesture. In some versions he is fully clothed, after the bourgeois Impressionist fashion; in others, like the women, he is naked. The group disport themselves in a green woodland light, the shapes of Nature repeating the angles of the man's formal dress and the comely shapes of the women. Within this lush, confined space Picasso concentrates his thoughts on the old, inexhaustible theme of the painter and his model, in which now the former and now the latter assert their personalities and presences, while the others in the group mind their own business or listen, if at all, with only half their minds. In the end it is the model who prevails. Picasso gives her a looming, monumental authority. Her beauty, her youth and her sex make the last, unequivocal statement.

During his years with Françoise Gilot, home for Picasso had been the unpretentious pink villa at Vallauris, called La Galloise. He

Plate 77
Peace
(detail)
1952
oil and gouache on plywood
Temple of Peace, Vallauris

divided his working time between La Galloise and the Paris house in the Rue des Grands Augustins. His celebrity grew to the point where he could no longer appear on the streets of Paris without strangers or journalists cornering him in encounters which caused Picasso increasing irritation and anxiety. Once Françoise was gone, La Galloise seemed a cheerless place; he resolved to find another base, to share with the devoted Jacqueline and to fill with his possessions.

His choice eventually fell on a roomy villa outside Cannes, known as La Californie. It was well screened by trees and, although not particularly elegant architecturally, blessed with excellent light and plentiful space. Without bothering to redecorate–a home to Picasso was essentially a place where a workman could get on with his job–he piled his books, pictures, scrap albums, souvenirs, sculptures, masks, pots, dogs, birds and goat into the empty rooms. Jacqueline presided over the *ménage*, which for long periods included Picasso's children Maïa (his daughter by Marie-Thérèse Walter), Claude and Paloma.

In this atmosphere he worked as steadily as ever, paying his own tribute to the house in paintings showing its comfortable spaces enclosed by arched shapes and widely spaced walls–'interior landscapes', as he called them. It was in La Californie, too, that Picasso embarked on the *Meninas* series, working day after day in the large attic he had chosen for the task. Hélène Parmelin, a frequent visitor, has described the demands which this commitment made of him. 'No sooner had he left the pigeon-loft studio than he began suffering from not being in it, and the whole of life and every evening were conditioned by it. But the next day, when the time came for work, he would go up to the studio as if mounting a scaffold.' To the south, this room commanded a view of the sea which Picasso painted (plate 91) framed by his window and by the pigeons who fluttered in and out all day, as welcome here as in his father's house in Málaga long ago.

Still the world made demands on him. Picasso found he could not move about freely, as he had been accustomed to do in Vallauris, chatting to neighbours, dropping into street cafés, making impromptu visits to public places, without attracting sightseers and autograph hunters. The beach was no longer a pleasure. The crowds and their noises intruded on La Californie. In search of a safer refuge, he bought the aristocratic Château de Vauvenargues, near Aix-en-Provence, on the slopes of Mont Ste Victoire: the landscape of Cézanne, whom Picasso venerated and who now, by a turn of fortune, re-entered his life as a *Zeitgeist*. In purchasing the Château de Vauvenargues, Picasso also became the owner of 2,000 acres and recipient, if he chose to use it, of an ancient title. In an effort to make himself feel at home, he plunged into a series of portraits of Jacqueline, who now became his wife.

In contrast to the austere seclusion of the Château de Vauvenargues, the work which Picasso did there is notably strong in both colour and emotion. The *Déjeuner* series, with its heightened emphasis on painterly tones and forms, was begun there; and a vibrant Spanish-ness distinguishes such works as the *Still-life with Mandolin* and *Woman with a Mirror*, both painted in June 1959. But Picasso was not to make much use of the château after that summer. Neither there nor at La Californie were conditions right for him: at Cannes, indeed, new hotels and apartment blocks soon obscured the views from the windows and overlooked the garden. Picasso heard from Paul Eluard of a villa five miles away, on top of a hill near Mougins, skirted by trees

Plate 78
Claude with His Hobbyhorse
1949
oil on canvas
$51\frac{1}{4} \times 38\frac{1}{4}$ in (130 × 97.1 cm)
Collection of the artist

Plate 79
Woman and Children Playing
1953
lithograph
$18\frac{7}{8} \times 24\frac{3}{4}$ in (48×63 cm)

and vineyards, called Notre-Dame-de-Vie after a nearby chapel. He bought it in April 1961, six months before his eightieth birthday – an event celebrated locally by feasting on a heroic scale, by a special exhibition of his paintings chosen by his friends, and by a bullfight and fireworks display. When it was all over and the last well-wisher had reluctantly taken his leave, Picasso went straight back to work.

He had renewed his interest in monumental sculpture, and was working in sheet metal as a means of achieving three-dimensional effects with flat surfaces, the spaces between the surfaces making the third dimension. By way of illustration of what he was after, he produced a large sheet of paper on which he had drawn a sprawling, unidentifiable shape, saying: 'That is a chair, and you see there an explanation of Cubism. Imagine a chair run over by a steam-roller – it would produce something like that.' Then he cut out the shape, folded the paper along lines which he had drawn on the surface, and stood it up. Re-made in flat metal sheets the paper cut-out became, unmistakably, a chair. He used the same principles to make a succession of highly inventive constructions, including several of a woman and child, a monkey, portrait heads, new versions of the *Man with a Sheep*, owls, cockerels, footballers (plate 92) – a gallery of brilliantly realised three-dimensional forms to which his brush added the final touch of identity. Though made on a small scale (they are only a few inches high) the sculptures could be enlarged to almost any size, a fact which enabled Picasso, when asked to produce a sculpture for the Chicago Civic Centre,

Plate 80
The Mask and the Monkey
1954
wash drawing
9½ × 12½ in (24 × 32 cm)

to make a maquette only 41 inches tall for a work destined to stand 50 feet high.

One of the most powerful of the many images which Picasso borrowed from earlier masters, *The Rape of the Sabine Women*, now found its way to the forefront of his imagination (plate 93). In the familiar versions by Poussin and David, the subject is treated as a classic set-piece in which the violence is set at a distance from the spectator, as if on a stage. Picasso's versions transform the narrative into brutally direct statements, ignoring the historical outcome, which was peace and forgiveness, in his insistence on a greater truth than mere story-telling: the barbaric savagery of the strong towards the weak. In one of the series, painted at Mougins between April and November 1962, the panic and clangour of the event are almost palpable as women and babies are strewn headlong and the abducted victims struggle naked in the arms of the riders, one of whom wears the red cap of a Jacobin. A colossal armed figure rears above the scene, his cleaver-like sword raised in menace. Between his legs an agonised mother who has been hurled to the ground with a baby in her arms stretches her head upwards in terror and entreaty. The din and drama are underlined in sour and vivid colours; the havoc is emphasised by scribbled strokes on walls, earth and sky.

In another version Picasso paints the mounted rider charging straight out of the canvas, the huge iron hoof arrested in the instant before crashing down on the helpless mother knocked dying in its path. The prominent male sex of the animal and the

exultant attitude of the rider proclaim the brutal masculinity of the crime. In a third version the onrushing horse and rider are challenged by a helmeted warrior; one of his armoured legs is braced on the body of a fallen woman, whose screaming child, a little girl, seems to be projecting herself upwards towards the dreadful action.

The intensity of Picasso's *Rape* series seems to have disconcerted some of his friends. Perhaps they were unprepared for such a burst of power in an artist over eighty years old, a man living apart from the everyday world of mass inhumanity. If so, they overlooked Picasso's lifelong concern with the drama of violence and death, his fascination for the *corrida*, and above all his moralistic notions of good and evil. 'To call up the face of war,' he said, 'I have never thought of any particular trait, only that of monstrosity . . . I am on the side of men, of all men. Because of that I could not imagine the face of war separated from that of peace . . . I would like my work to help men to choose, after having forced them to recognise themselves according to their authentic calling, among my images. So much the worse for those who are constrained to recognise themselves in pictures of war . . .' Even more than with the *Meninas*, the *Rape of the Sabine Women* made demands on him which seemed at times unsupportable. 'It has never been like this,' he told Hélène Parmelin. 'It's the most difficult thing I have ever done.'

As he entered into the last decade of his life, Picasso again found

Plate 82
The Dance
1954
lithograph
$18\frac{7}{8} \times 25\frac{1}{4}$ in (48 × 64 cm)

his thoughts turning to the insoluble relationship between the artist and his model: the microcosm of men's relationships with women, of men's with other men, and of women's with other women, enhanced yet made more mysterious by Picasso's deliberate identification of art with life, so that the act of painting becomes itself the subject of painting. Had he not said all this before? Was his work not finished after more than seventy-five years? 'No,' Picasso said. 'There is never a moment when the painter can say, "I have done a good day's work and tomorrow is Sunday" . . . You can never write the words The End.'

Between February and June 1963 he completed 45 paintings on the theme of the artist and the model, on some occasions as many as three or four in a day. He shows the painter as a man at home, in his environment, surrounded by his familiar objects, wearing his familiar clothes, doing his job. But exactly what he is doing is not shown; the interest lies between the painter and the woman who, for the moment, has all his thoughts as he tries to transfer her to his canvas. Her nudity interests him only incidentally: her sex is explicit, but since nakedness is total the artist is no more concerned with it than with any other manifestation of her identity. Picasso was insistent that he wished to paint nudes 'only as they are'. 'I want to *say* a nude. I don't want to make a nude like a nude.' Let the spectator get what he likes out of his images of women. 'You want a couple of breasts? Right, here you are. Let the fellow looking at it have everything handy that he needs for making a nude. If you provide him with these things he will put them in place himself with his eyes. Everyone will make just the nude he wants with the one I make for him.'

Often the model in Picasso's painting is indeed on this level, an Identikit figure, and the painter would not begrudge any spectator the pleasure of re-assembling the parts in some private image of his own. But the real model is much more: she is a presence, a collaborator, a loved one, a muse. Sometimes she looks like Jacqueline, at other times like some squatting African idol. Or she is a bride, or she reclines like Goya's *Maja* in the studio or in a landscape where the painter wears a broad-brimmed hat against the sun and holds a mask to his face. The permutations follow one another with urgency and excitement: Picasso, absorbed in a private reappraisal, makes a public statement on the most persistent theme of his life.

And still Picasso could not say, 'Tomorrow is Sunday.' Jacqueline reappears, nude with a small black cat, seeming with her gesture to command the artist's attention; or as a strongly modelled *Seated Nude*, the planes of her body stated in areas of blank canvas set against swirling, luminous tones of yellow and flame.

Turning to graphic art, Picasso produced between 1966 and 1968 a quantity of drawings which, by excluding the dimension of colour, force attention on to the calligraphic statements of his pen. The figures are sometimes disguised in costume, which serves to heighten the *comédie humaine* effect of the anecdotes in which they take part. Mere humans consort with immortals; the painter turns into Velázquez or brandishes a twig instead of a paintbrush; the *dramatis personae* of the bullfight appear once more, the *torero* in the role of the painter thoughtfully running his eye over a young woman escorted by a duenna, or over a whore stripping off in his presence. The Man with a Sheep meets a nude woman and a boy playing a flute, on the beach; the woman starts to eat a watermelon; the sheep stops struggling; a cockerel turns up to listen. The artist reappears in his studio, visibly ageing (plate 94); the piper arrives, and the model stretches languorously to his music or closes her eyes in bliss. Nude men and women ride in on the backs of donkeys, followed by a portly figure on a goat who finds Cupid fondling a dove. Suddenly we are at the circus, with clowns and bare-back (more properly bare-bottom) riders watched by ranks of solemn spectators. Several sheets are crowded with figures seen in different lights, some classically clear in outline, others in silhouette. In a few the hatching is so dense that the detail can only be guessed at.

Plate 83
Portrait of Jacqueline
1955
ceramic
diameter 16½ in (42 cm)
Private collection

Picasso himself makes an entrance on all fours, a naked woman sitting on his head, pursued by Cupid with a drawn bow. Now he, or an *alter ego*, is found in a brothel inspecting at close quarters, but without emotion, the women's private parts. The female matador is seen again, now bereft of her costume as she sprawls across the back of her horse, dead, a magnet for men's eyes. A series of men's faces, staring out of the picture from a nervous tangle of crayon lines, fix the spectator with a half-pleading, half-troubled stare. Then we are back in the circus with Jacqueline being carried round the ring on a white horse, watched by a young man whose profile, seen as a shadow, registers enjoyment at the sight of her flesh. A man and a woman struggle for intimacy through their mouths; too close to focus on each other's faces, their eyes stare wildly above the grappling teeth and tongues. A handsome strumpet wearing only a necklace, a descendant of the *Courtesan* of 1901, is unveiled by a sexually excited, androgynous attendant for the owner of a pair of eyes peering over the veil (plate 95).

Next we are in a harem, where a lounging sultan enjoys the sight of a houri with a fluttering bird perched on her finger, who in another drawing shares her couch with a handsome goat. This sequence leads to a reminiscence of the voluptuous female bathers of Ingres (plate 96), whom Picasso draws in attitudes of mutual

Plate 84
Portrait of Jacqueline
1957
oil on canvas
$45\frac{3}{4} \times 35$ in (116×89 cm)
Museo Picasso, Barcelona

admiration, reclining, swimming, putting up their hair. In one of the series a young girl enviously views the bodies of the women, her arms folded across her unripened breast. After a long series of drawings in which a gallantly costumed man contemplates a reclining nude, sometimes with an aged crone on guard, Picasso returns to the allegory of the circus and the ballet in which men and women dress up without really concealing themselves.

All through the series, spread over three years, there are references to themes and details in his earlier work. Picasso himself steals in and out of the scene, sometimes in disguise, sometimes in a youthful reincarnation, sometimes as the grizzled veteran of many a bordello, looking and remembering. The painter and model theme is developed to a more universal confrontation: man faces woman, woman faces man. But they do

Plate 85
Sylvette
1955
oil on canvas
$31\frac{3}{4} \times 25\frac{1}{4}$ in (81 × 64 cm)
Kunsthalle, Bremen

not touch. The space between them may be charged with curiosity and desire but Picasso shows no sign, at this point, of crossing it. One wonders if the next frame in the long cartoon will ever be drawn.

Suddenly it is; and in a manner which releases all tensions in a series of witty explosions. In March 1968 Picasso embarked on a series of etchings in which, using much the same cast as in the drawings, he stages an outright Saturnalia. The artist, now in the garb of Raphael, mounts his startled model on the studio couch, still holding a brush in one hand and palette in the other. In a version a few days later, a bearded face peers from under the rug, registering concern or perhaps disapproval. In other plates the model stimulates the painter with erotic posturings. Rembrandt appears, looking interested (plate 97). Picasso, self-caricatured as an aged midget, plays the role of spectator or *voyeur*. The party gathers pace; more women join in, their limbs spreadeagled, their sex proclaimed like exclamation marks.

The etchings liberate the paintings. Now the painter may embrace his model, the man his woman: not with chastity, since for Picasso art was never chaste, nor with any sense of shame – since 'only when painting isn't really painting can there be an affront to modesty' – but with carnality and love.

The activity of Picasso's last years is awesome. It is as if his life was rushing towards a climax, not an end. To mark his eighty-fifth birthday the French government organised an international exhibition of his paintings, consisting of over 500 works, in Paris. Five years later, at ninety, he became the first painter to be given a one-man exhibition in the Louvre during his lifetime. Meanwhile he carried on working. Between March and October 1968 he made 347 etchings and other prints (plate 98), as well as a dozen etchings and aquatints published at Mougins as illustrations to a book. His entire output of 140 paintings done in 1969 was exhibited at the Palais des Papes in Avignon as part of the 1970 festival, and created a sensation.

The paintings at Avignon, strung unceremoniously around the ancient walls, as naked as when they left the studio, were a triumphantly virile summing-up of a life's work. Every one of them was the recent work of a man who, by the normal laws of nature, should by now have laid aside curiosity, impudence and eroticism, saving his remaining energies for the fight against physical and mental decay. Instead, the impact was one of superb

Plate 86
Eugène Delacroix
Women of Algiers
1834
oil on canvas
71 × 90¼ in (180 × 229 cm)
Louvre, Paris

Plate 87
The Women of Algiers
1955
oil on canvas
$47\frac{3}{4} \times 57\frac{1}{2}$ in (115 × 146 cm)
Collection of Mr and Mrs Victor W. Ganz,
New York

authority, in which wit, sensuality and violence were indivisibly joined, as in earthly potentates since the beginning of time. The 200 works presented a statement as complete and unequivocal as the noble stones on which they hung. What might have seemed pretentious in almost any other artist of our time appeared here as a conjunction of natural forces on a magnified human scale. Each painting, complete in its own terms, addressed itself to the spectator, some cryptically, others ironically or with delight. Every one was of humanity, looking, touching, gesticulating, wondering, joined or estranged in tense spaces: the matador, the painter, old men, children, grandees, models, their eyes and hands, limbs and genitals charged with electrifying power.

Picasso produced some 200 drawings in 1970, and uncounted

others in 1971 and 1972. By then the Museo Picasso in Barcelona was the richer by three priceless bequests: the Picasso family's collection of his earliest works, lovingly preserved from his boyhood and student days; the collection of his friend Jaime Sabartés; and the *Meninas* studies and paintings, which Picasso personally donated, along with the attendant 'pigeon' series, in 1968. After his death in April 1973 his estate was conservatively estimated at £50 million, by far the greatest fortune ever amassed by any artist, and nearly all consisting of his own works. His name was known around the world, as familiar as Coca-Cola. It was, and remains, a synonym for what millions of people, most of whom have never seen a Picasso painting, mean by 'modern art'.

Picasso himself had little patience with talk of 'art': 'It's Art that kills us. People no longer want to do painting: they make Art, and they are given it. But the less Art there is in painting the more painting there is.' His distinction between painting and art is a distinction between work and something which is less real. Picasso's achievement is to have brought new concepts of reality, the

Plate 88
Diego Velázquez
Las Meninas
1656
oil on canvas
125 × 108½ in (318 × 276 cm)
Prado, Madrid

products of work, to almost the entire range of visual and plastic arts: to painting, drawing, printmaking, sculpture, pottery, in whatever materials lay to his hand. But the nature of this reality has nothing to do with the discoveries which, in Picasso's lifetime, transfigured the material world. Nowhere in his work does he seek significance in the machines and gadgetry of our times. There are no aeroplanes or motor cars, moon rockets or mushroom clouds in Picasso. To him, the appurtenances of life in the 20th century had no pictorial or associative relevance in themselves. The external forces which bear on men's lives are not shown, any more than the bombs which fell on the people of Guernica. The painter's search for reality, according to Picasso, is of a totally different kind. 'You can go to the moon or walk under the sea, or anything you like, but painting remains painting because it eludes such investigation. It remains there like a question. And it alone gives the answer.'

Serious painters are usually content to let their work speak for them; indeed Picasso would never admit any other basis of

Plate 89
Las Meninas
1957
oil on canvas
$76\frac{3}{4} \times 102\frac{1}{4}$ in (194 × 260 cm)
Museo Picasso, Barcelona

Plate 90
Le Déjeuner sur l'Herbe
1961
pencil
10⅝ × 14½ in (27 × 37 cm)

critical evaluation, or acknowledge the interpretations of particular works offered by his friends. He rarely gave his paintings titles: the ones which have become accepted were for the most part suggested by one or other of his circle, or by cataloguers. One picture might be more successful than another in evoking a response in people, but that did not necessarily make it more important. In any case, Picasso was always reluctant to regard a painting as finished; for him, once it had been brought to that state it was as good as dead. He would keep paintings in his studio for months, even years, in case at some time he felt the need to change or add to them. He signed only when he parted with them, and from that moment they held little further interest for him. 'Why should I go?' he said, when invited to a major retrospective exhibition of his work. 'I have seen them all before.'

Critical analysis of Picasso's work is brought up short by this unconcern for objective values. He simply did not care if he was looked on as some kind of mutation, an improbable freak. He told Dor de la Souchère: 'I am like the giraffe which doesn't know that it is monstrous. The appraisal comes from the other side of the bars.' This is not to say that he was insensitive to criticism, only to disbelief. For the greater part of his career he was beyond the reach of hostile reviewers, secure in a market which he understood very well and had no hesitation in profiting from. All his life he numbered among his friends some of the most articulate critical writers of the time – Guillaume Apollinaire, Max Jacob, André Breton, André Salmon, Louis Aragon, Paul Eluard, André Malraux – whose judgments on his work illuminate some aspects